DIRECTORY TITLE WRITER...

UTILITIES

Val J. Golding

Produced by:
Brian Wiser & Bill Martens

 Apple PugetSound Program Library Exchange

Directory Title Writer

www.callapple.org

ISBN: 978-1-387-89312-6

ACKNOWLEDGEMENTS

Directory Title Writer was created by Val J. Golding in 1981.

Message Output section written by Andy Hertzfeld.

PRODUCTION

Brian Wiser → Design, Layout, Editing, Cover
Bill Martens → Scanning, Layout, Disk Updates

DISCLAIMER

About Val J. Golding

Val J. Golding founded Apple Pugetsound Program Library Exchange (A.P.P.L.E.) in 1978 with the help of Mike Thyng and Bob Huelsdonk at the suggestion of Max Cook, a manager at the ComputerLand where Val bought his Apple II.

Val also wrote for *Softdisk*, *On-three* and other technology magazines over the years primarily making his mark in the early years of Apple computing.

As the founder, Val was instrumental in guiding the company to the position it is in now. Val was the Managing Editor of *Call-A.P.P.L.E.* magazine and also served as the chairman of the board of directors.

His wife and daughters were a big part of documenting his stories about his hobby of Cable Cars, and he was the editor of a highly acclaimed newsletter for his daughter's school. He passed away at age 77 on July 2, 2008 after a long battle with cancer.

About the Producers

Brian Wiser

Brian Wiser is a producer of books, films, games, and events, as well as a long-time consultant, enthusiast and historian of Apple, the Apple II and Macintosh. Steve Wozniak and Steve Jobs, as well as *Creative Computing*, *Nibble*, *InCider*, and *A+* magazines were early influences.

Brian designed, edited, and co-produced dozens of books including: *Nibble Viewpoints: Business Insights From The Computing Revolution*, *Cyber Jack: The Adventures of Robert Clardy and Synergistic Software*, *Synergistic Software: The Early Games*, *The Colossal Computer Cartoon Book: Enhanced Edition*, *All About Applesoft: Enhanced Edition*, *Graphically Speaking: Enhanced Edition*, *What's Where in the Apple: Enhanced Edition*, and *The WOZPAK: Special Edition* – an important Apple II historical book with Steve Wozniak's restored original, technical handwritten notes. Brian is also the author of *The Etch-a-Sketch and Other Fun Programs*.

He passionately preserves and archives all facets of Apple's history, and noteworthy companies such as Beagle Bros and Applied Engineering, featured on AppleArchives.com. His writing, interviews and books are featured on the technology news site CallApple.org and in *Call-A.P.P.L.E.* magazine that he co-produces as an A.P.P.L.E. board member. Brian also co-produced the retro iOS game *Structris*.

In 2005, Brian was cast as an extra in Joss Whedon's movie *Serenity*, leading him to being a producer and director for the documentary film *Done The Impossible: The Fans' Tale of Firefly & Serenity*. He brought some of the *Firefly* cast aboard his Browncoat Cruise and recruited several of the *Firefly* cast to appear in a film for charity. Throughout these experiences, he develops close personal relationships with many actors, authors, and computer industry luminaries. Brian speaks about his adventures to large audiences at conventions around the country.

Bill Martens

Bill Martens is a systems engineer specializing in office infrastructures and has been programming since 1976. The DEC PDP 11/40 with ASR-33 Teletypes and CRT's were his first computing platforms with his first forays in the Apple world coming with the Apple II computer.

Influences in Bill's computing life came from *Byte* magazine, *Creative Computing* magazine, and *Call-A.P.P.L.E.* magazine as well as his mentors Samuel Perkins, Don Williams, Joff Morgan, and Mike Christensen.

Bill is the author of *ApPilot/W1*, *Beyond Quest*, *The Anatomy of an EAMON*, and multiple EAMon adventure games, as well as a co-producer of many books including *What's Where in the Apple: Enhanced Edition*, *The WOZPAK: Special Edition*, *Nibble Viewpoints: Business Insights From The Computing Revolution*, and co-programmer for the iOS version of the retro game *Structris*. He has written many articles which have appeared in user group newsletters and magazines such as Call-A.P.P.L.E..

Bill worked for Apple Pugetsound Program Library Exchange (A.P.P.L.E.) under Val Golding and Dick Hubert as a data manager and programmer in the 1980s, and is the current president of the A.P.P.L.E. user group established in 1978. He reorganized A.P.P.L.E. and restarted *Call-A.P.P.L.E.* magazine in 2002. He is the production editor for the A.P.P.L.E. website CallApple.org, writes science fiction novels in his spare time, and is a retired semi-pro football player.

CONTENTS

INTRODUCTION: The Wonderful Wizard of DOS   1

OPERATION: Somewhere Over the Catalog   3

  (A) Feature Selection   3

    1. DIRECTORY SECTOR NUMBER   3

    2. CHANGE LINK   4

    3. CHANGE ANY BYTE   4

    4. TITLE NUMBER   4

    5. DELETE A FILE   5

    6. TITLE ENTRY MODE   5

    7. CHANGE TRACK/SECTOR LIST POINTER TO $11,01   6

    8. CHANGE FILE TYPE   6

    9. CHANGE SECTOR COUNT   7

  (B) Entry Screen Display   8

  (C) Sector Display/Write to Disk   9

UTILIZATION: Follow the Yellow Byte Road   11

  (A) Ideas and Suggestions   11

    1. HIDING A FILE   11

    2. DUMMY FILES   11

    3. CONTROL CHARACTERS   12

    4. USING CHANGE A BYTE   12

  (B) Memory Map   13

Program Source   15

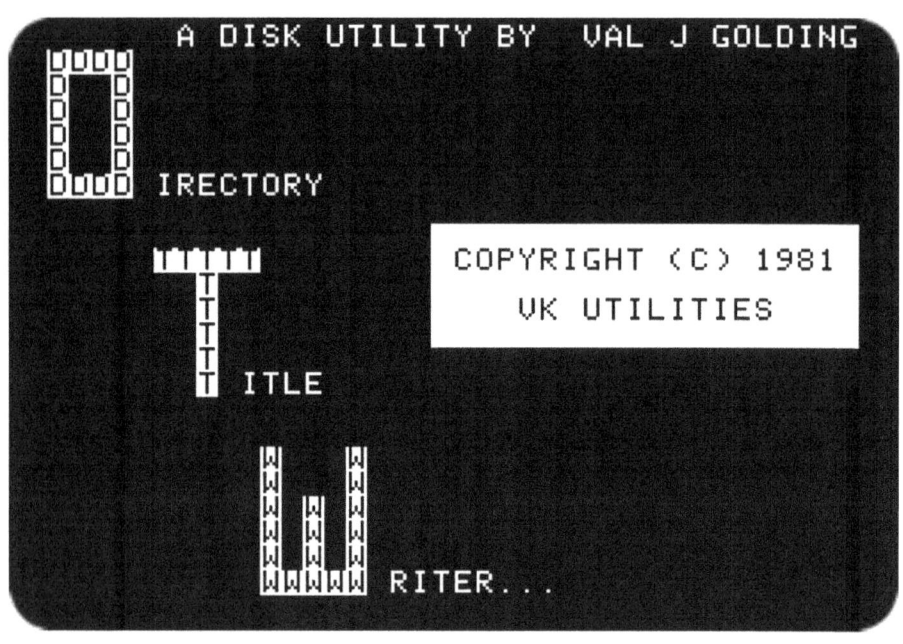

A DISK UTILITY BY VAL J GOLDING

DIRECTORY

TITLE

WRITER...

COPYRIGHT (C) 1981
VK UTILITIES

INTRODUCTION:
The Wonderful Wizard of DOS

by Val J. Golding

It started with Clif Howard's excellent article on "Directory Title Formatting" which appeared as the feature article in the July-August 1980 *Call-A.P.P.L.E.*, a need for a utility that would permit the direct entry on a diskette of fancy and/or illegally-formatted file names [directory titles], and to which article we refer you for additional information on the structure of the VTOC (Volume Table of Contents) and directory sectors. See also pages 129 to 131 of Apple's DOS 3.2 or DOS 3.3 manual.

Directory Title Writer is just such a utility. It was written as a time saver, and to facilitate the entry of "dummy" titles [files] to the diskette catalog to produce a "pretty" formatted header, such as those used by A.P.P.L.E. and other organizations. The manual creation of a fancy header on a single diskette can take as much as two hours by laboriously writing the titles out on paper, converting each ASCII character to the appropriate hex value and then typing the hex bytes in with a disk edit utility such as *Disk Zap*, and finally writing the changes to a diskette. *Directory Title Writer* will do the same job in a matter in minutes.

It is designed for ease of use, and to the extent possible, maximum use is made of error-trapping on user input. It is completely self-prompting, with a warning before any data is written to disk, giving the user an opportunity to re-check his work and abort if needed. Certain user-selected parameters are optional in one set of circumstances, and mandatory in another. Wherever mandatory, they are automatically entered by default. Default provisions have been made for all entry parameters (except Write a Byte.) The entry screen displays at all times all essential instructions and current parameter data.

In addition, certain supplemental features have been added which are not essential to writing a file name, but may prove helpful in making other changes to a directory sector. These provisions allow changing (a) the directory sector link bytes, (b) any single byte in the sector specified by the user, and (c) deleting a file, even one which does not

1

yet exist. The supplemental features, taken along with the other provided functions, make *Directory Title Writer* a complete directory sector management system.

The original purpose of *Directory Title Writer* was to assist in the formatting of commercial diskettes, but it is equally suited to many additional uses, limited only by the user's imagination. It can be used for example, to "hide" a filename from view on the catalog through the inclusion of 7 or 8 Control-H's (backspaces), yet the hidden program can be loaded by another program, using the Applesoft CHR$ function in a string. It could also be used to rename a file name that has hidden control characters in it.

```
   THIS PROGRAM ALLOWS YOU TO ENTER YOUR
OWN DIRECTORY TITLES FROM THE KEYBOARD,
IN FLASH, INVERSE OR NORMAL, UPPER OR
LOWER CASE. FOLLOWING MAY BE SPECIFIED:

SECTOR NO:           [RANGE (1-C, 1-F)]
CHANGE LINK:         [C/R=N]
CHANGE ANY BYTE:     [C/R=N]
TITLE NO.:           [RANGE (1-7)]
DELETE A FILE:       [C/R=N]
DISPLAY:             [C/R=NORMAL]
U/L CASE:            [C/R=UPPER]
CHANGE T/S POINTERS TO 11,1: [C/R=Y]
CHANGE FILE TYPE:    [C/R=N]
CHG SECTOR COUNT TO 0: [C/R=Y]

        HIT ANY KEY TO CONTINUE
```

2

OPERATION:
Somewhere Over the Catalog

Directory Title Writer is run by booting the diskette on DOS 3.2 or DOS 3.3, whichever is appropriate. A separate diskette is required for 13 or 16 sector operation, as the program may not be Muffined from 3.2 to 3.3.

After booting, an opening title panel is displayed, advising the user of the expected entry parameters and options. Nine choices are available as follow:

1. Directory sector number
2. Change link
3. Change any byte
4. Title number within the sector
5. Delete a file
6. Title entry mode
7. Change track/sector list pointer
8. Change file type
9. Change sector count

Each feature is described in further detail in the following section.

(A) Feature Selection

1. DIRECTORY SECTOR NUMBER

This is the sector of the catalog you wish the new or modified file name to be written to. If you are starting with a newly initialized diskette, it would normally be $C ($F for DOS 3.3). A directory normally commences in Sector $C ($F) of Track $11, and decrements as each sector becomes filled. The last available sector is $1. Entries therefore must be within the range $C-$1 ($F-$1 for DOS 3.3). Entry of any other value returns the user to the prompt.

2. CHANGE LINK

This is a supplemental feature which allows the user to change the two bytes in a sector that normally show a link to the next lowest numbered directory sector. This feature should be used only by one who has sufficient knowledge of DOS and the directory to understand its implications. Changing the link to point to other than the next lowest numbered sector can cause portions of the directory to be skipped when cataloged. Setting the link pointers to 0,0 will tell DOS "This is the end of the directory." Any key other than "Y" defaults to the "No" condition and proceeds to the next prompt. If "Y" is selected, the user will be prompted to input first the track number, followed by the sector number to be pointed to by the link. Once the link has been changed, the program jumps to the Sector Display/Write to Disk routine.

3. CHANGE ANY BYTE

Another supplemental feature, Change a Byte allows the user to specify any byte within the sector that is desired to be changed, and the value for that byte. This is handy, in that it may be used, for example, to make a one byte correction in a title, or to change any byte not directly accessed by other routines in this program. CAUTION is urged, since any provision for error checking would negate the potential of this routine. Default for this feature is "N", and the user moves to the next prompt. If Change a Byte is selected, the routine jumps to the Sector Display/Write to Disk routine.

4. TITLE NUMBER

This is a sequential number for the seven possible titles within a directory sector. Normally a "1" would be chosen if starting with a new diskette. Any number outside the range 1-7 will return the user to the prompt. If a sector and title is selected where an active or deleted file exists, the file name will be displayed, and the user will be asked whether or not it should be replaced. Default on this input is "N", therefore any response other than "Y" will proceed to the Delete File routine, and ultimately to the Write Next Title prompt. A "Y"

4

response will lead to the Delete routine and then jump to Title Entry Mode.

5. DELETE A FILE

This feature permits the user to "delete" a file name, even when one does not exist. It is provided in order that the user may wish to, for example, place dummy titles in sector $B, while reserving space in Sector $C for real files that will be added at a later time. DOS will not display an active file name unless it is preceded by active or deleted files .

When DOS deletes a file, it takes the track number from the track/sector list pointer at relative byte $00, replaces it with a $FF, and moves it to relative byte $20, the last byte of the now deleted file name. This routine performs an identical operation. If "Y" is selected, the file, whether it exists or not, is deleted, and we jump to Write Next Title. The default condition of the delete routine is "N" and will lead to Title Entry Mode, unless the user has previously opted to not replace an existing file, in which case we jump to Write Next Title.

6. TITLE ENTRY MODE

This feature controls the form in which the file name will ultimately appear on the catalog, i.e., whether it will be in inverse video, flashing video or normal, (upper or lower case) video. Selection of the three primary modes is by entering I, F or N, as appropriate. The default mode is normal. If normal is selected, the user will be asked to enter a "Y" (or any other character) for upper case, a "N" for lower case. Default is to upper case.

Control characters except Control-M may be entered at any time from any mode. If inverse mode has been selected, they will display on the entry panel as flashing. If any other mode has been selected, they will be displayed in inverse video.

No editing may be performed while in entry mode, as the forward and reverse arrow keys are used for other functions.

When in either inverse or flashing entry mode, the ESCape key will cause the next character entered to be in normal mode. When entering in lower case, the ESCape key will cause the next character entered to be upper case.

7. CHANGE TRACK/SECTOR LIST POINTER TO $11,01

Each time a new file is created on a diskette, DOS assigns a minimum of two sectors for that file (one in the case of text files). The first sector assigned is where the actual track/sector list [sub-directory] is stored, and pointers to this list are maintained in the catalog sector.

This feature allows setting the track/sector list pointers to $11, 01 for a dummy file. Since $11, 01 has already been allocated to the directory, no additional disk space will be used. If the user writes a file name to a sector and title number previously unused, this feature is automatically invoked. If overwriting a previously existing file name, the user has the option of changing or not changing the pointers. Any character other than "N" will default to the change.

8. CHANGE FILE TYPE

Six file types may be displayed on a diskette directory: A, B, I, R, S, T, representing Applesoft, Binary, Integer, Relocatable Binary, Special, and Text. "R" files are applicable to DOS 3.3 only, and "S" files are not currently assigned, although this feature can change and display either. Any character entered, other than the six listed above, will return the user to the Change File Type input. File locking must be done manually.

Table of File Types:

```
Hex Value:  00 01 02 04 08 10
FileType:    T  I  A  B  S  R
```

Add $80 for locked files.

6

9. CHANGE SECTOR COUNT

The effect of this option, which changes the sector count to 0, is cosmetic only, and has no bearing on the requirements of DOS. If a new file name is being entered, the change is automatic. Any key other than "N" will default to the "Y" option.

(B) Entry Screen Display

After the final feature has been selected, except in the case of the Change Link, Delete File, or the following information will be displayed on the screen, where xxxxx indicates variable data:

```
ENTER TITLE DATA BETWEEN BRACKETS
TRAILING NORMAL SPACES NEED NOT BE ENTERED
HIT ESCAPE FOR A NORMAL CHARACTER (if in inverse or
flash). HIT ESCAPE TO CAPITALIZE (if in lower case)
ENTER CONTROL CHARACTERS ANYTIME
ARROW KEYS MAY NOT BE USED

          TITLE DISPLAY MODE: xxxxx
          CURRENT SECTOR:     xx
          CURRENT TITLE NO.:  xx
          TRACK/SECTOR LIST:  xx, xx
          FILE TYPE:          x
          SECTOR COUNT:       xx

  [-----------------------------------------------]
```

The screen display will remain as long as the user is entering data. A maximum of 30 characters may be used in a file name. Trailing spaces in normal mode need not be entered. Trailing normal spaces in inverse or flash mode need not be entered. When the 30th character is typed, or when a carriage return or a Control-M is entered, the first title will be completed and the title counter will be incremented. If it is less than 8, the user will be prompted "ENTER NEXT TITLE (Y/N)". A "Y" response will return the user to the Entry Display Mode, described above. Any key other than "Y" will default to "No", clear the screen and format it to display the entire sector, described in the following section. If the title counter is equal to 8, then the program automatically proceeds to Sector Display/Write to Disk.

(C) Sector Display/Write to Disk

When the user has indicated that no further data is to be written, or when seven titles have been entered, the screen will be cleared and a dual format display of the subject sector will be provided. The upper third of the screen will show the modified sector in ASCII characters, with each file name appearing as it will when the disk is cataloged. In addition, control characters will be shown in inverse video, as will other non-title data from the sector, except that the inverse "@" will not be displayed. The lower 2/3 of the screen show the sector as a hex dump in the form two bytes, then a space, two more bytes, etc., 16 bytes per line.

This total screen display affords the user an opportunity to double check the accuracy of all entries to date before writing to the disk. The last line of the screen displays an inverse video prompt "WRITE TO DISK (Y/N)". This is the point of no return. A "Y" response will write the new data to the disk and then ask if the user wants to enter data in a new sector. A "N" response to the question "Write to Disk," which is also the default condition, will result in the loss of all previously entered data.

When the data has been written to disk, or when a "N" response has been entered to the "Write to Disk" prompt, the user will be asked whether or not data is to be entered to a new sector. A "N" response, the default condition, will return the user to MONITOR, and the diskette must be rebooted to run the program again. A "Y" response returns to the Sector Number prompt near the beginning of the program.

UTILIZATION:
Follow the Yellow Byte Road

(A) Ideas and Suggestions

1. HIDING A FILE

A file name can be hidden from view on the catalog, yet RUN by another program. The hidden file should be the last file on the directory or else a blank line will show where the file name would normally print. A program file may begin with a non-alpha character. However, while it can be LOADed, BLOADed, RUN or BRUN, DOS will not SAVE or BSAVE a file name beginning with a non-alpha character. If we create a file named "A" and wish to hide it, we must follow the "A" with eight backspaces. The following Applesoft program would RUN the program name we have just created:

```
100  D$ = CHR$(4)
110  FOR I= I TO 8: FILE$ = FILE$ + CHR$ (8): NEXT
120  FILE$= "A" + FILE$
130  PRINT D$"RUN"; FILE$: END
```

2. DUMMY FILES

Seven backspaces will create a blank line in the catalog.

Seven backspaces followed by any combination of characters will create a file whose name begins on the leftmost position of the screen, as long as the file is unlocked. None of the file attributes will show.

Good judgement should be used when entering a title in lower case. Remember, not everyone has a lower case adapter, in which case the title would appear as "garbage" characters.

3. CONTROL CHARACTERS

Most control characters may be entered into any title, and they will be acted upon by the Apple Monitor. A Control-H [backspace) may also be entered with the left Arrow Key. A Control-J will produce a line feed and a Control-M will produce a carriage return/line feed. However, DOS will not know about these two characters and may not scroll the catalog as you expect. A Control-M may not be written directly, as the program will interpret it as a carriage return. It must be inserted as $8D using the Change a Byte routine. Remember to leave a space for it.

4. USING CHANGE A BYTE

This module was developed so the user could access any byte in the directory sector that was not included in the other routines. Some examples of its use could be:

- Undelete a file
- Insert a Control-M [Carriage Return]
- Change the Track/Sector List pointers to other than $11, 01
- Change the sector count to other than zero, or as it now exists.
- Correct an error in a file name
- Intermix flash and inverse characters within one title

Use of this routine requires knowledge of how the directory sector is structured. This is explained in the *DOS Manual*, and a memory map appears in the following section. A detailed chart of Apple II Video Display Characteristics may be found on page 15 of the new *Apple II Reference Manual*.

(B) Memory Map

A DOS 3.2 or 3.3 directory sector is divided into eight sections. Each of the eight sections are set off by heavy vertical rules on the memory map. The first section, which is just 11 ($A) bytes long, contains only the next sector link, with the track in byte 2 and the sector in byte 3. All other bytes are unused. The remaining seven sections are 35 ($23) bytes long, and are used by each of the seven allowable titles. One file name section consists of the following:

1st byte	Track No. of Track/Sector list
2nd byte	Sector No. of Track/Sector list
3rd byte	File type
4th to 33rd bytes	Actual file name (30 characters)
34th byte	Sector count
35th byte	End mark (always a zero)

If a file has been deleted, the first byte will be changed to $FF and the 33rd byte will contain the former contents of the first byte. If the two link bytes in the first section are changed to zeroes, this indicates to DOS that the current sector is the final sector of the directory. A table of significant locations in a directory sector follows:

	Track	Sector	File Type	1st Byte Title	30th Byte Title	Sector Count	End Mark
Relative Byte	00	01	02	03	20	21	22
Title 1	0B	0C	0D	0E	2B	2C	2D
Title 2	2E	2F	30	31	4E	4F	50
Title 3	51	52	53	54	71	72	73
Title 4	74	75	76	77	94	95	96
Title 5	97	98	99	9A	B7	B8	B9
Title 6	BA	BB	BC	BD	DA	DB	DC
Title 7	DD	DE	DF	E0	FD	FE	FF

13

The complete Directory Sector Memory Map:

LSB\MSB	00	01	02	03	04	05	06	07	08	09	0A	0B	0C	0D	0E	0F
00	-	TK	SEC	-	-	-	-	-	-	-	-	TK	SEC	FT	1	1
01	1	1	1	1	1	1	1	1	1	1	1	1	1	1	1	1
02	1	1	1	1	1	1	1	1	1	1	1	1	S CNT	E MK	TK	SEC
03	FT	2	2	2	2	2	2	2	2	2	2	2	2	2	2	2
04	2	2	2	2	2	2	2	2	2	2	2	2	2	2	2	S CNT
05	E MK	TK	SEC	FT	3	3	3	3	3	3	3	3	3	3	3	3
06	3	3	3	3	3	3	3	3	3	3	3	3	3	3	3	3
07	3	3	S CNT	EMK	TK	SEC	FT	4	4	4	4	4	4	4	4	4
08	4	4	4	4	4	4	4	4	4	4	4	4	4	4	4	4
09	4	4	4	4	4	S CNT	EMK	TK	SEC	FT	5	5	5	5	5	5
0A	5	5	5	5	5	5	5	5	5	5	5	5	5	5	5	5
0B	5	5	5	5	5	5	5	5	S CNT	EMK	TK	SEC	FT	6	6	6
0C	6	6	6	6	6	6	6	6	6	6	6	6	6	6	6	6
0D	6	6	6	6	6	6	6	6	6	6	6	S CNT	EMK	TK	SEC	FT
0E	7	7	7	7	7	7	7	7	7	7	7	7	7	7	7	7
0F	7	7	7	7	7	7	7	7	7	7	7	7	7	7	S CNT	EMK

Program Source

```
*
*
*
 AST 32
*                                    *
*                                    *
*     DIRECTORY TITLE WRITER         *
*                                    *
*        BY   VAL J. GOLDING         *
*                                    *
*                                    *
*        COPYRIGHT (C) 1981          *
*           VK UTILITIES             *
*                                    *
 AST 32
*
*
MEMPTR = $0
IOB = $3
DOSFLG = $5
DRVNO = $6
TEMP = $7
TPLUS = $1B
CH = $24
CV = $25
A1L = $3C
A1H = $3D
A2L = $3E
A2H = $3F
A4L = $42
A4H = $43
INVFLG = $32
PROMPT = $33
*
*
BASIC = $3D0 BACK TO BASIC WITH DOS
RWTS = $3D9
GETIOB = $3E3
MEMCALC = $3D5
```

15

```
SLOT = $5F8
*
*
KBD = $C000
STROBE = $C010
PRBL2 = $F94A
VTAB = $FC22
HOME = $FC58
RDKEY = $FD0C
GETLN = $FD6A GET LINE OF CHRS
CROUT = $FD8E OUTPUT A C/R
PRBYTE = $FDDA PRINT HEX OF A
COUT = $FDED OUTPUT A CHAR
MOVE = $FE2C
SETINV = $FE80
SETNORM = $FE84
RESET = $FF59
GETNUM = $FFA7 GET A NBR
ZMODE = $FFC7
*
*
* DIRECTORY BUFFER OFFSETS
*
TLST = $4
SCCNT = $22
ENDMK = $21
TTLLNG = $23
*
*
*
 ORG $7000
*
*
*
PGMST LDA #$FF
 STA CHGSEC
 STA ACTIVE
 LDA #$0
 STA SC
*
*
```

```
*
* This clever bit of code looks at
* A6B3 which holds a zero in 3.2 DOS
* and non-zero in 3.3.  It then sets
* the variable DOSFLG accordingly.
*
 LDA MEMCALC CHECK MEMORY SIZE
 ADC #$9 OFFSET TO HI BYTE OF
 STA MEMPTR+1 LOCATION TO CHECK.
 LDA #$B3 LO BYTE
 STA MEMPTR
 LDY #$0
 LDA (MEMPTR),Y
 BNE NOT13 IF NON ZERO, IT'S 3.3
 LDA #$D
 STA DOSFLG
 BPL START
NOT13 LDA #$10
 STA DOSFLG
*
*
START JSR GETIOB FIND DOS'S I/O BLOCK
 STA DRVNO+1
 STY DRVNO
 LDY #$10
 LDA (DRVNO),Y GET LAST DRIVE NBR USED
 STA DRVNO FILE IT, MAY NEED AGAIN
*
 JSR TITLE
 JSR HOME
 JSR INTRO PRINT OPENING TITLES
 JSR INIT SET UP OUR OWN I/O BLOCK
*
*
*
Q1 JSR MSGOUT
 ASC '  SECTOR NBR ? '
 HEX 00
 JSR MSGIN
 STA IBSECT PUT IT IN THE IOB
 BEQ Q1
```

```
 CMP DOSFLG CHECK WHICH DOS VERSION
 BGE Q1
 JSR RDSEC
 JMP LINK
Q2 JSR MSGOUT
 ASC '  TITLE NBR ? (1-7) '
 HEX 00
 JSR MSGIN
 STA DIRTTL
 BEQ Q2 ZERO IS A NO-NOO
 CMP #$8 NEITHER IS 8 OR MORE
 BGE Q2
 JSR CROUT
*
*
* This is where we check to see if the
* title number specified is an active file.
* If so, best ask user if he wants to
* replace it with his own title.
*
*
TFINDST JSR GETOFF
 CLC
 LDY DIRTTL
 LDA OFFSET
 ADC #ENDMK-1
TFIND DEY
 CPY #$0
 BNE TFIND
 LDA OFFSET
 TAY
 LDA SECTBUF,Y
 STA ACTIVE
 BEQ Q3
*
*
*
 JSR TLMSG
 JMP HEXOUT+3 DISPLAY THE FOUND TITLE
*
*
```

18

```
BACK LDA ACTIVE
 BPL REAL
 JSR MSGOUT
 ASC '] IS DELETED.  REPLACE IT ? (Y/N) '
 HEX 00
 JSR CHRIN
 CMP #"Y"
 BEQ Q3A
 JMP Q7
*
*
REAL JSR MSGOUT
 ASC ']   IS ACTIVE.  REPLACE IT ? (Y/N) '
 HEX 00
BACK1 JSR CHRIN
 CMP #"Y"
 BEQ Q3A
 JMP Q3
*
*
*
Q3 JMP DELETE
 JSR CROUT
Q3A JSR DISMSG
 JSR MSGOUT ASK FOR DISPLAY MODE
 ASC '(I/F/N) ? '
 HEX 00
 JSR CHRIN
 CMP #"I"
 BEQ IMODE
 CMP #"F"
 BEQ FMODE
 JMP CASE
IMODE LDA #$3F SET MODE FLAG
 STA MODE FOR INVERSE
 BPL Q4
FMODE LDA #$7F OR FLASH
 STA MODE
 BPL Q4
*
CASE JSR CROUT
```

```
 JSR MSGOUT
 ASC '  UPPER CASE ONLY ? (Y/N) '
 HEX 00
 JSR CHRIN
 CMP #"N"
 BNE NMODE
 LDA #$80 SET MODE FLAG FOR NORMAL U/CASE
 STA MODE
 BMI Q4
NMODE LDA #$FF OR LOWER
 STA MODE
Q4 LDA ACTIVE
 BEQ Q5-3
 JSR CROUT
 JSR MSGOUT
 ASC '  CHANGE T/S PTR ? (Y/N) '
 HEX 00
 JSR CHRIN
 JSR CHGTS GO FIX IT
Q5 NOP
 NOP
 JSR CHGFT
Q6 LDA ACTIVE
 BEQ Q6A
 JSR MSGOUT
 HEX 8D
 ASC '  SECTOR COUNT=0 ? (Y/N) '
 HEX 00
 JSR CHRIN
 JSR CHGSC FIX THIS ONE, TOO
Q6A JMP ENTER
*
 HEX 8D8D00
MODEMSG LDA MODE
 BMI MODEMSG1 IF NORMAL
 JSR MSGOUT
 ASC '  HIT ESC TO ENTER A NORMAL CHARACTER.'
*
*
* This is the section that formats the
* screen for title data entry and lets
```

```
* the user know in which display mode
* the data is being entered.  After
* reading the proper sector into a buffer,
* the new data is stored in the buffer
* and written back to the disk.
*
 HEX 8D00
MODEMSG1 JSR CROUT
 JSR BLANK
 JSR DISMSG
 LDA MODE
 CMP #$7F
 BEQ FTITLE
 CMP #$3F
 BEQ ITITLE
 JSR MSGOUT
 ASC 'NORMAL'
 HEX 8D00
 RTS
*
*
*
*
ITITLE STA INVFLG
 JSR MSGOUT
 ASC 'INVERSE'
 HEX 8D00
 LDA #$FF
 STA INVFLG
 RTS
*
FTITLE STA INVFLG
 JSR MSGOUT
 ASC 'FLASH'
 HEX 8D00
 JSR SETNORM
 RTS
*
*
*
*
```

```
ENTER JSR HOME
 JSR MSGOUT
 HEX 8D8D
 ASC '  ENTER TITLE DATA BETWEEN BRACKETS'
 HEX 8D
 ASC '  TRAILING SPACES NEED NOT BE ENTERED.'
 HEX 8D00
 PLA
 LDA MODE
 CMP #$80 CHECK FOR LOWER CASE
 BNE FORMAT
 JSR MSGOUT
 ASC '  Hit ESCape to capitalize'
 HEX 8D00
 JMP FORMAT
*
*
FORMAT JSR MSGOUT
 ASC '  ENTER CONTROL CHARACTERS ANY TIME'
 HEX 8D
 ASC '  ARROW KEYS <- -> MAY NOT BE USED.'
 HEX 8D00
 JSR MODEMSG
 JSR CURSEC
 JSR CURTTL
 JSR TSMSG
 JSR FTMSG
 JSR SCMSG
FORMAT1 JSR MSGOUT
 HEX 8D8D8D8D
 ASC ' [_____]          '
 HEX 00
 LDA #$2
 STA CH
 CLC
 LDA OFFSET
 ADC #TLST-1
 TAX
 LDY #$0
*
*
```

```
* Here is where the dirty work is done;
* all conversions are made and the
* user's character is stored away.
*
CHRLOOP JSR RDKEY
 CMP #$8D
 BEQ FINISH
 CMP #$9B
 BEQ CAP
 CMP #$A0
 BLT CTLCHR
 JSR MODECHK
 PLA
STORE STA SECTBUF,X
 JSR COUT
 INX
 INY
 CPY #32
 BEQ Q7
 JMP CHRLOOP
CTLCNV PLA
 SEC
 SBC #$80
 JMP STORE+3
CTLCHR STA SECTBUF,X
 PHA
 LDA MODE
 CMP #$3F
 BNE CTLCNV
 PLA
 SEC
 SBC #$40
 JMP STORE+3
FINISH LDA #$A0
SPACE STA SECTBUF,X
 INX
 INY
 CPY #$20
 BNE SPACE
 JMP Q7
*
```

```
CAP JSR RDKEY GET THE NEXT CHR AFTER AN 'ESC'
 JMP STORE AND STORE IT IN THE BUFFER
*
Q7 INC DIRTTL
 LDA DIRTTL
 CMP #$8 IF TITLE = 8, WE NEED
 BEQ DS TO DISPLAY THE SECTOR AND FINISH
 PHA
 JSR MSGOUT
 HEX 8D8D
 ASC 'WRITE NEXT TITLE ? [NBR '
 HEX 00
 PLA
 JSR PRBYTE
 JSR MSGOUT
 ASC '] (Y/N)'
 HEX 00
 JSR CROUT
 JSR CHRIN
 CMP #"Y"
 BNE DS
 JSR GETOFF
 JMP TFINDST
DS LDX #$FF
 JMP HEXOUT
*
*
*
* This section checks the MODE flag
* and then makes the proper conversions.
*
RGER JMP STORE-1
*
*
MODECHK PHA
 LDA MODE
 CMP #$FF
 BEQ RGER
 CMP #$80
 BEQ LCASE
 CMP #$7F
```

```
 BNE INVTITLE
 PLA
 CMP #$C0
 BLT NONALPH
INVCNV SEC
 SBC #$80
 JMP STORE ;+3 DOES ZERO WORK?
INVNTALF SEC
 SBC #$80
 JMP STORE
*
NONALPH SEC
 SBC #$40
 JMP STORE
*
INVTITLE PLA
 CMP #$C0
 BLT INVNTALF
 SBC #$C0
 JMP STORE
*
*
LCASE PLA
 CMP #$C0
 BGE ALPHA
 JMP STORE
*
*
ALPHA CLC
 ADC #$20
 JMP STORE
*
*
GETOFF LDY #$7
 STY TEMP
 LDA #$FF
 SEC
 SBC #TTLLNG
TLLOOP CPY DIRTTL
 BEQ SUBTR
 DEY
```

```
 BPL TLLOOP
*
SUBTR CPY TEMP
 BEQ SUBDONE
 SEC
 SBC #TTLLNG
 DEC TEMP
 JMP SUBTR
*
SUBDONE STA OFFSET
 INC OFFSET
 RTS
*
*
*
TLMSG JSR HOME
 JSR MSGOUT
 ASC 'TITLE ['
 HEX 00
 LDA OFFSET
 CLC
 ADC #$3 DON'T DISPLAY FIRST THREE BYTES
 LDX #ENDMK-3 OFFSET X TO COME OUT EVEN
 TAY
 RTS
*
*
*
* OUTPUT ROUTINES
*
*
*
*
*
HEXOUT JSR HOME
 LDA SECTBUF,Y
 BEQ SKIPCHR DON'T DISPLAY ZEROS,
 CMP #$80
 BLT THRU
 CMP #$A0
 BGE THRU
```

```
 SEC
 SBC #$40
THRU JSR COUT
 CPX #$FF TRICK TO CONFUSE THE X-REG
 BEQ INY
 DEX ;USED ONLY BY THE REPLACE? ROUTINE
 BEQ RTX
INY INY
 CPY #$0
 BNE HEXOUT+3
 JSR CROUT
 LDY #$0
*
*
* This section does the hex dump --
* prints two bytes, then a space.
*
NXTHEX LDA SECTBUF,Y
 JSR PRBYTE
 INY
 LDA SECTBUF,Y
 JSR PRBYTE
 LDA #$A0
 JSR COUT
 INY
 CPY #$0
 BNE NXTHEX
 JMP MORE
RTX JMP BACK
*
*
REPLACE DEX
 BNE INY
 JMP BACK
*
SKIPCHR LDA #$A0
 JMP THRU
*
*
*
CHGSC TAX
```

```
 CLC
 LDA OFFSET
 ADC #SCCNT-1
 TAY
 TXA
 CMP #"Y"
 BEQ FIXIT
 LDA SECTBUF,Y
 STA SC
 RTS
FIXIT LDA #$0
 STA SC
 STA SECTBUF,Y
 RTS
*
*
*
*
CHGTS TAX
 LDA ACTIVE
 BNE CHGTS1
 LDX #"Y" FORCE A CHANGE
CHGTS1 LDA OFFSET
 TAY
 TXA
 CMP #"Y"
 BNE NOFIX
 LDA #$11
 STA SECTBUF,Y
 STA TL
 INY
 LDA #$01
 STA SECTBUF,Y
 STA SL
 JSR SAVEFT
 RTS
NOFIX LDA SECTBUF,Y
 STA TL
 INY
 LDA SECTBUF,Y
 STA SL
```

```
       JSR SAVEFT
       RTS
*
*
CHGFT JSR CROUT
      JSR MSGOUT
      ASC '  CHANGE FILE TYPE ? (Y/N) '
      HEX 00
      JSR CHRIN
      CMP #"Y"
      BNE NOTHNX
      JSR CROUT
      JSR MSGOUT
      ASC '  FILE TYPE OPTIONS: (A/B/I/R/S/T) '
      HEX 00
      JSR CHRIN
      STA FTASCII
      LDY #$0
FF CMP FTYPE,Y
      BEQ GOTIT
      INY
      CPY #$11
      BLT FF
      BPL CHGFT
GOTIT STY FTHEX
      TYA
      LDY TPLUS
      STA SECTBUF,Y
      BPL RTS
*
NOTHNX LDA ACTIVE
      BNE YES
      LDA #$D4
      STA FTASCII
      BMI RTS
*
YES LDY TPLUS
      LDA SECTBUF,Y
      CMP #$80
      BLT NXTOP
      SEC
```

29

```
 SBC #$80
NXTOP STA FTHEX
 TAY
 LDA FTYPE,Y
 STA FTASCII
*
RTS RTS
*
*
*
*
SAVEFT INY
 STY TPLUS
 LDA SECTBUF,Y
 STA FTHEX
 RTS
*
*
*
LINK JSR MSGOUT
 ASC '  CHANGE LINK ? (Y/N) '
 HEX 00
 JSR CHRIN
 CMP #"Y"
 BEQ CHLINK
 JSR CROUT
 JMP ANY
CHLINK JSR CROUT
 JSR MSGOUT
 ASC '  TRACK ? '
 HEX 00
 JSR MSGIN
 CMP #$23
 BGE CHLINK
 LDY #$1
 STA SECTBUF,Y
 INY
CHLINK1 JSR CROUT
 JSR MSGOUT
 ASC '  SECTOR ? '
 HEX 00
```

```
 JSR MSGIN
 CMP DOSFLG
 BGE CHLINK1
 STA SECTBUF,Y
 LDX #$FF
 JMP HEXOUT
*
*
*
ANY JSR MSGOUT
 ASC '  CHANGE ANY BYTE ? (Y/N) '
 HEX 00
 JSR CHRIN
 CMP #"Y"
 BEQ ANYBYTE
 JSR CROUT
 JMP Q2
ANYBYTE JSR CROUT
 JSR MSGOUT
 ASC '  BYTE TO CHANGE ? (0-FF) '
 HEX 00
 JSR MSGIN
 PHA
 JSR CROUT
 JSR MSGOUT
 ASC '  DATA FOR BYTE ? '
 HEX 00
 JSR MSGIN
 TAX
 PLA
 TAY
 TXA
 STA SECTBUF,Y
 LDX #$FF
 JMP HEXOUT
*
*
*
DELETE JSR CROUT
 JSR MSGOUT
 ASC '  DELETE THIS FILE ? (Y/N) '
```

31

```
 HEX 00
 JSR CHRIN
 CMP #"Y"
 BEQ KILLIT
 JSR CROUT
 LDA ACTIVE
 BNE DELETE1
 JMP Q3A
DELETE1 JMP Q7
KILLIT LDA OFFSET
 TAY
 LDA SECTBUF,Y
 PHA
 LDA #$FF
 STA SECTBUF,Y
 TYA
 ADC #ENDMK-2
 TAY
 PLA
 STA SECTBUF,Y
 LDX #$FF
 JMP Q7
*
*
*
*
*
*
*
BLANK LDX #$5 PRINT 5 SPACES
 JSR PRBL2
 RTS
*
*
*
TITLE JSR HOME
 LDA #>SECTBUF
 ADC #$1
 STA A1H
 CLC
 ADC #$4
```

```
 STA A2H
 LDA #<SECTBUF
 STA A1L
 STA A2L
 LDA #$04
 STA A4H
 LDA #$0
 STA A4L
 JSR MOVE
 JSR CHRIN
 RTS
*
*
*
*
* INITIALIZE IOB, ETC.
*
INIT LDY #<IOBLOCK+1 Here is where store the
 LDA #>IOBLOCK+1 parameters required by
 STY IOB our own I/O block.
 STA IOB+1
 LDA #$11
 STA IBTRK
 LDA DOSFLG
 STA IBSECT
 LDA #<DCT
 STA IBDCTP
 LDA #>DCT
 STA IBDCTP+1
 LDA #<SECTBUF
 STA IBBUFP
 LDA #>SECTBUF
 STA IBBUFP+1
 LDA #$1
 STA IBCMD
 LDA #$0
 STA IBSTAT
 LDA SLOT
 STA IOBPSN
 STA IBSLOT
 LDA DRVNO
```

33

```
 STA IOBPDN
 STA IBDRVN
 RTS
RDSEC LDY IOB GIVE RWTS IOB ADDRESS
 LDA IOB+1 IN Y AND A REGS
 JSR RWTS CALL RWTS FOR FIRST READ
 JSR ERRMSG
 RTS
*
*
*
*
ERRMSG BCS ERRCK IF CARRY SET WE HAD AN ERROR
 RTS
*
*
ERRCK LDA IBSTAT
 PHA
 LDA #$0
 STA IBSTAT
 STA CV
 JSR VTAB
 JSR BLANK
 PLA
 CMP #$10
 BEQ WPERR
 JSR MSGOUT
 ASC '  FATAL ERROR * DISK I/O '
 HEX 87878D00
 JMP BASIC
*
*
WPERR JSR MSGOUT
 ASC '   WRITE PROTECT ERROR '
 HEX 87878D00
 PLA
 JMP MORE
*
*
*
*
```

```
*
MORE JSR BLANK
 JSR SETINV
 JSR MSGOUT
 ASC ' WRITE SECTOR TO DISK (Y/N)? '
 HEX 00
 JSR SETNORM
 JSR CHRIN
 CMP #"Y"
 BEQ WRITE
 JMP NEWSEC
WRITE JSR HOME
 LDA #$2
 STA IBCMD
 LDY IOB
 LDA IOB+1
 JSR RWTS
 JSR ERRMSG
*LDA #1
 DEC IBCMD ;Restore read flag
*
*
*
NEWSEC JSR CROUT
 JSR MSGOUT
 ASC '  WRITE NEW SECTOR ? (Y/N) '
 HEX 00
 JSR CHRIN
 CMP #"Y"
 BNE NOPE
 JSR HOME
 JMP Q1
*
NOPE JSR HOME
 JMP BASIC
*
*
*
*
*
DISMSG JSR CROUT
```

```
 JSR MSGOUT
 ASC '  TITLE DISPLAY MODE: '
 HEX 00
 RTS
*
*
 JSR CROUT
*
*
CURSEC JSR CROUT
 JSR BLANK
 JSR MSGOUT
 ASC '  CURRENT SECTOR:     '
 HEX 00
 JSR SETINV
 LDA IBSECT
 JSR PRBYTE
 JSR SETNORM
 JSR CROUT
 RTS
*
*
CURTTL JSR BLANK
 JSR MSGOUT
 ASC '  CURRENT TITLE:     '
 HEX 00
 JSR SETINV
 LDA DIRTTL
 JSR PRBYTE
 JSR SETNORM
 JSR CROUT
 RTS
TSMSG JSR BLANK
 JSR MSGOUT
 ASC '  TRACK/SECTOR LIST: '
 HEX 00
 JSR SETINV
 LDA #"$"
 JSR COUT
 LDA TL
 JSR PRBYTE
```

```
 LDA #","
 JSR COUT
 LDA #$A0
 JSR COUT
 LDA SL
 JSR PRBYTE
 JSR SETNORM
 JSR CROUT
 RTS
*
*
FTMSG JSR BLANK
 JSR MSGOUT
 ASC '   FILE TYPE:           '
 HEX 00
 JSR SETINV
 LDA FTASCII
 NOP
 JSR COUT
 JSR SETNORM
 JSR CROUT
 RTS
*
*
SCMSG JSR BLANK
 JSR MSGOUT
 ASC '   SECTOR COUNT:        '
 HEX 00
 JSR SETINV
 LDA SC
 JSR PRBYTE
 JSR SETNORM
 JSR CROUT
 RTS
*
*
*
*
*
*
*
```

```
* MESSAGE OUTPUT BY ANDY HERTZFELD
*
*
MSGOUT PLA
 STA TEMP
 PLA
 STA TEMP+1
 LDY #0
LOOP INC TEMP
 BNE SKIPADD
 INC TEMP+1
SKIPADD LDA (TEMP),Y GET CHR
 BEQ MSGRTS CHR=0, END OF STRING
 ORA #$80
 JSR COUT OUTPUT CHR
 JMP LOOP
MSGRTS LDA TEMP+1 RESET RTS TO AFTER
 PHA
 LDA TEMP
 PHA
 RTS
*
*
CHRIN BIT STROBE
KEY BIT KBD KEYPRESS?
 BPL KEY NO
 LDA KBD YES, SAVE IN ACC
 BIT STROBE
 JSR COUT
 RTS
*
*
*
MSGIN LDA #$A0
 STA PROMPT
 LDX #$0 This subroutine gets a string
 JSR GETLN of ASCII characters representing
 JSR ZMODE hex, converts each two chrs to a
 JSR GETNUM single byte, and returns
 JSR CROUT it in A2L
 LDA A2L
```

```
 RTS
*
*
INTRO JSR MSGOUT
 HEX 8D8D
PGMEND ASC '  THIS PROGRAM ALLOWS YOU TO ENTER YOUR'
 HEX 8D
 ASC 'OWN DIRECTORY TITLES FROM THE KEYBOARD,'
 HEX 8D
 ASC 'IN FLASH, INVERSE OR NORMAL, UPPER OR'
 HEX 8D
 ASC 'LOWER CASE. FOLLOWING MAY BE SPECIFIED:'
 HEX 8D8D
 ASC 'SECTOR NO:        [RANGE (1-C, 1-F)]'
 HEX 8D
 ASC 'CHANGE LINK:      [C/R=N]'
 HEX 8D
 ASC 'CHANGE ANY BYTE:  [C/R=N]'
 HEX 8D
 ASC 'TITLE NO.:        [RANGE (1-7)]'
 HEX 8D
 ASC 'DELETE A FILE:    [C/R=N]'
 HEX 8D
 ASC 'DISPLAY:          [C/R=NORMAL]'
 HEX 8D
 ASC 'U/L CASE:         [C/R=UPPER]'
 HEX 8D
 ASC 'CHANGE T/S POINTERS TO 11,1: [C/R=Y]'
 HEX 8D
 ASC 'CHANGE FILE TYPE:  [C/R=N]'
 HEX 8D
 ASC 'CHG SECTOR COUNT TO 0: [C/R=Y]'
 HEX 8D8D00
 JSR BLANK
 JSR BLANK
 JSR SETINV
 JSR MSGOUT
 ASC 'HIT ANY KEY TO CONTINUE'
 HEX 8D8D00
 JSR SETNORM
 JSR CHRIN
```

```
 JSR HOME
 RTS
 BRK
*
*
*
*
* DATA FOR I/O BLOCK AND DCT
*
* This is where we set up our very own
* I/O Block, just like the one DOS has.
*
*
IOBLOCK NOP ;LABEL THE IOB
IBTYPE HEX 01 ALWAYS
IBSLOT DS 1 SLOT# * 16
IBDRVN DS 1 DRV # THIS ACCESS
IBVOL HEX 00 VOL NBR EXPECTED
IBTRK DS 1 TRK # THIS ACCESS
IBSECT DS 1 SEC # THIS ACCESS
IBDCTP DS 2 POINTERS TO DCT
IBBUFP DS 2 POINTERS TO SECTOR BUFFER
 HEX EAEA NOT USED
IBCMD HEX 01 0=NULL 1=READ 2=WRITE 4=FORMAT
IBSTAT HEX 00 10=WRPRT 20=VLMM 40=DRER 80=RDER
IBSMOD DS 1 VOL # FOUND
IOBPSN DS 1 LAST SLOT ACCESSED
IOBPDN DS 1 LAST DRIVE ACCESSED
*
*
* DEVICE CHARACTERISTICS TABLE
*
DCT HEX 00 DEV CODE TYPE (00)
 HEX 01 PHASES PER TRK (01)
 HEX EFD8 TIMING COUNT
*
* MISCELLANEOUS STORAGE AREA
*
*
OFFSET DS 1
CHGSEC DS 1
```

```
DIRTTL DS 1
SECNUM DS 1
MODE DS 1
TL DS 1
SL DS 1
FTP DS 1
SC DS 1
FTHEX DS 1
*
*
FTASCII HEX D4
FTYPE HEX D4C9C1FFC2
 HEX FFFFFFD3
 HEX FFFFFFFFFFFFFFD2
ACTIVE HEX FF
*
*
 DS $11 ;Set buffer to page boundary
NOP NOP ;Title screen BLOADs here + $100
SECTBUF = NOP ;Pgm hangs w/o mem move
* may store false data in page 4 scratch pads
 LST OFF
```

www.ingramcontent.com/pod-product-compliance
Lightning Source LLC
Chambersburg PA
CBHW051255170526
45165CB00004B/1721